A

D1417891

Aaseng, Nate
Kirby Puckett

SPORTS GREAT
KIRBY
PUCKETT

—Sports Great Books—

SPORTS GREAT
KIRBY
PUCKETT

Nathan Aaseng

—Sports Great Books—

ENSLOW PUBLISHERS, INC.

Bloy St. & Ramsey Ave. P.O. Box 38
Box 777 Aldershot
Hillside, N.J. 07205 Hants GU12 6BP
U.S.A. U.K.

To Jay, Maury, Mikhaila and
to Evan, whose first words were "Kirby Puckett"

Library of Congress Cataloging-in-Publication Data
Aaseng, Nathan.
　　Sports great Kirby Puckett / Nathan Aaseng.
　　　　p. cm. — (Sports great books)
　　Includes index.
　　ISBN 0-89490-392-6
　　1. Puckett, Kirby—Juvenile literature. 2. Baseball players—
United States—Biography—Juvenile literature. I. Title.
II. Series.
GV865. P83A27 1993
796.357'092—dc20
[B]

　　　　　　　　　　　　　　　　　　　　92-38433
　　　　　　　　　　　　　　　　　　　　CIP
　　　　　　　　　　　　　　　　　　　　AC

Printed in the United States of America

10 9 8 7 6 5 4 3 2 1

Photo Credits:
Scott Aaseng, p. 15; AP / Wide World Photos, pp. 10, 32, 40; Boston Red Sox, p. 44;
California Angels, p. 23; National Baseball Library, Cooperstown, NY, p. 28; Rick Orndorf/
Minnesota Twins, pp. 12, 18, 25, 30, 33, 36, 47, 50, 55, 57, 59.

Cover Photo: Rick Orndorf / Minnesota Twins

Contents

Chapter 1

Kirby Puckett, looking for all the world like a cuddly bear, scurried to the plate in Milwaukee's County Stadium on August 19, 1987. Nothing in this short, bulky man's appearance warned that he was a dangerous hitter. He showed no menacing scowls, no fierce glint in his eye, no cool swagger to his step. Puckett waved his bat eagerly—nervously—like a kid who could hardly wait to start tearing into his pile of birthday presents. Milwaukee pitcher Len Barker, though, saw nothing cute about the batter who faced him. He knew that the innocent-looking Puckett was one of baseball's most dangerous hitters.

Over the years American League pitchers had learned that Puckett was about as fond of walks as a cat is of baths. Few batters were as determined as Puckett to take their swings. Sometimes Puckett was so eager to hit that he would swing at balls far out of the strike zone. Lately he had been doing just that and had been hitting the ball poorly. Barker would try to take advantage of such eagerness and get Puckett to chase a bad pitch.

Puckett knew very well what was coming. After going hitless in four at bats the previous night, he had gone to his batting coach for advice. Puckett knew that his team could not afford to have him in a slump. The Minnesota Twins had lost nine of their last ten games. They had fallen into a first-place tie with the Oakland A's. What could Puckett do to stop the Twins' slide? Coach Tony Oliva had told him two things: stop taking strikes early in the count, and stop swinging at high fastballs out of the strike zone.

With Oliva's advice fresh in his mind, Puckett laid off Barker's high fastball in the first inning. He waited for a better pitch and drove the ball into the outfield for a single. That hit primed the pump. In the third inning Puckett smashed another Barker pitch into the seats for a solo home run. The Twins now had a 3–1 lead over the Brewers.

Two innings later Puckett took his turn against a new pitcher, Ray Burriss. The muscular little center fielder pounded out another home run to make the score 4–2. An inning later he whacked a single and scored another run as the Twins broke away to a 12–3 win. Two home runs and two singles in five at bats would have been a season's highlight for many major leaguers. But Puckett was just building up steam.

The next afternoon Puckett, wearing his familiar number 34, came to bat in the first inning with two men on base and nobody out. He drilled a single off Milwaukee lefty Juan Nieves to score a run. In the third inning Puckett blasted his third solo home run in two days. Nieves had one last chance at Puckett in the fifth inning, but Kirby stroked another single off him.

In the middle of his impressive batting show, Puckett showed that he was equally as flashy with a baseball glove. With bases loaded in the sixth inning, Milwaukee's Robin Yount launched a drive to deep center field. Puckett raced back toward the fence. As the ball started its downward arc, he thought there was a chance he might have room to catch it. Puckett jumped high. Just as the ball cleared the fence, headed for the seats, Puckett speared it. This catch turned Yount's grand slam home run into a long out!

Then Puckett went back to work with the lumber. He smashed two doubles off reliever Chuck Crim—in the sixth and again in the eighth. With two outs in the ninth, the Brewers gave Puckett one last chance. The team's catcher dropped a third strike and allowed Greg Gagne to reach first base. That gave Kirby Puckett one last chance to bat—against All-Star fireballer Dan Plesac.

By this time Puckett's batting explosion had won the admiration of the opposing fans. As Kirby stepped up to the plate the Brewer fans cheered him on. "I heard a lot of fans clapping for me," Puckett said. "I just went up and tried to do my best."

Plesac fired a perfect pitch, low and away. But, as Plesac later remarked, "A guy like him gets hot, he hits everything." Somehow Puckett lifted the low pitch deep into the right field seats for a home run to seal a 10–6 Twins' win.

The shell-shocked Brewers' pitching staff was more than ready to bid goodbye to Puckett. In two games the Brewers had retired him only once. Puckett had pounded out 10 hits, tying a major league record for most hits in consecutive games. None of them were cheap hits, either. Every ball had been hit hard—four of them leaving the ballpark.

Kirby Puckett's two-day batting spree did more than boost his own statistics. It recharged the sputtering Twins just when the team was starting to slip out of the divisional race. Minnesota stormed back into sole possession of first place and cruised to the first World Series title in the team's history.

Outside Minnesota few baseball enthusiasts in 1987 knew

Puckett drills one of his record-tying six hits in one game against the Brewers.

why Twins' fans were going crazy over this lovable, oddly-shaped center fielder. Since then Puckett has shown the entire country why he is one of baseball's special athletes. Despite a long series of spectacular seasons, Puckett's manner at the plate has not changed. He still acts as if each at bat is a special birthday present. He looks exactly like what he is—a person who is tickled to death to be out on a ballfield. "Ever since I was five I just wanted to play baseball," remembers Puckett. "The game was fun as a kid; it's fun now!"

The game is too much fun for Puckett to think about his own ego. Even after a bad day at the plate, he celebrates a team victory as joyfully as the rest of the team. "We won, I'm having fun," he said with a smile after going hitless in a Twins' win. Rather than expecting special treatment because he is a star, Puckett shows up two weeks early for spring training. He starts the season off with his head freshly shaved so "the boys can rub my head and relax. Someone's got to be the good luck charm." What other superstar in sports lets his teammates occasionally treat him like a team mascot?

Puckett's playful attitude has helped make the Twins a hard-working, close-knit team. Nobody feels like loafing when the team star is working his tail off. Personality clashes don't have much room to develop when the star is such a lovable sort. Puckett is a gentle soul who gets along with everyone. Once when asked what television show he hated the most, he replied, "I don't hate anything . . . that's too harsh a word for me."

Kirby Puckett brings an extra something to the game of baseball. Sports have become serious business in our world. Author George Will emphasized the point when he entitled his recent book on baseball players *Men at Work*. But Kirby Puckett in a baseball uniform hardly looks like a man punching a time clock. Watching him scamper around the

Showing the all-out hustle that has earned him respect throughout the league, Puckett barrels into the shortstop to break up a double play.

field like a frisky rookie, it's impossible to think of baseball as a job or an entertainment business. Puckett reminds everyone that baseball is a game, and that games are supposed to be fun. No wonder that Puckett has become the most popular Twins player of all time. Opposing manager Dick Williams was speaking for legions of fans across the country when he said, "I just love watching Kirby Puckett play."

Chapter 2

Kirby Puckett now lives comfortably in one of the wealthier neighborhoods of suburban Minneapolis. The world that he wakes up to each day is almost entirely different from the world into which he was born on March 14, 1961.

Puckett spent the first twelve years of his life in the Robert Taylor housing project on Chicago's South Side. The neighborhood was every family's nightmare. High-rise apartments piled poverty and despair on top of more poverty and despair. The Robert Taylor homes were so overrun with crime and drug dealings that *Newsweek* magazine once called them the "place where hope died."

Not even this bleak setting, however, could kill the hope in the youngest of the nine Puckett children. "I was a kid enjoying myself," Kirby Puckett remembers. As far as he was concerned he was living a normal childhood. He went to school, came home to the Pucketts' fourteenth-floor apartment, did his homework, and then looked for kids to play with.

Most of the time he had baseball on his mind. "Ever since

A section of the Robert Taylor Homes in which Puckett spent his early years.

I was five I just wanted to play baseball," Puckett has said. It was not always easy to find a place to play the game. Kirby often had to content himself with throwing a ball against a wall or hitting rolled up socks in his room.

As he grew older he began to play by the garbage bins in the back of the apartments. But it was a tough neighborhood and Puckett was not always left in peace. Once some bullies grabbed his baseball and hit it over the expressway that ran behind the apartments. It was one of the few times that the usually cheerful Kirby ran home in tears.

Until he reached the age of 12 Puckett lived less than a mile away from Comiskey Park, the home of the Chicago White Sox. But he followed Chicago's other baseball team, the Cubs. Ernie Banks and Billy Williams were his favorite Cubs. His idol, however, was San Francisco Giant outfielder Willie Mays. Mays had no weakness as a player. He had great home run power, yet hit for high average as well. Mays could steal bases, field well, and throw well.

"I remember hearing an announcer say Mays was a complete player," said Puckett. "That's what I wanted to be."

Unfortunately Puckett was always one of the smaller boys in his class. By the time he reached high school, he realized that he would never grow very tall. "I decided that if I was going to be short, I was going to have some muscle." The skinny Puckett began drinking protein supplements to help put on weight. And he started lifting weights in hopes of pumping himself up to look like bodybuilder Arnold Schwarzeneggar.

After the Pucketts moved out of the projects, Kirby attended Calumet High School. There he worked his way into a starting position on the baseball team. He was fast and a good fielder, and he usually made contact with the bat. But his strength-building program took a while to produce results. Although he was one of the team's star players, Puckett rarely hit anything longer than a single. Pro scouts took one look at this 5 foot, 8 inch singles hitter and rejected him as too small for the big leagues.

With his baseball career apparently going nowhere, Puckett looked for jobs to support himself. After high school graduation he was hired by the Ford Motor Company to work on a factory assembly line. After a short time at Ford, he joined the U.S. Census Bureau.

But despite what the scouts were telling him, he did not give up on his lifelong dream to play baseball. In the summer of 1980 Puckett showed up at a free agent tryout put on by a scout for the Kansas City Royals. Again Puckett failed to impress the pros, but he did catch the eye of one observer. Bradley University baseball coach Dewey Kalmer was not as choosy as the pro scouts. Kalmer could see why Puckett was not getting any pro offers. His small, thick body looked strange for a ballplayer—especially on top of those small, size 8-$\frac{1}{2}$ feet. "He was a short-armed third baseman who swung at everything," Kalmer said. "He was not a good player, but he was fast."

Kalmer could also see that Puckett was packing a lot of muscle on his short frame. The combination of speed, power, and enthusiasm made Puckett an interesting prospect. Kalmer persuaded Puckett to attend Bradley University in the fall of 1980. He then switched Puckett from third base to center field to take better advantage of his speed.

Kalmer's new find developed more quickly than anyone expected. In his first season at Bradley, Puckett earned a spot on the All-Missouri Valley Conference first team.

Puckett's time at Bradley, however, was cut short by family tragedy. Kirby's father, a postal worker, suffered a heart attack near the end of the school year. When his father died Kirby decided to move to a college closer to where his

Pro scouts had said that Puckett was too small to be a professional ball player. In 1982 the Twins decided to take a chance, and made him the third pick of the free agent draft.

mother lived. He transferred to Triton Community College in River Grove, Illinois.

In between schools Puckett played baseball in an Illinois summer college league. The Minnesota Twins' assistant farm director, Jim Rantz, had a son playing in that league. He took some time off from his duties one day to watch Mike Rantz in action. The temperature during one game climbed to more than 90° F. The heat took its toll on the players, who moved sluggishly in the field. But Jim Rantz noticed one oddly built player prancing around the bases as fresh and cool as a bubbling spring. If Kirby Puckett was even aware of the heat, he was not showing it. He blasted a home run and a double, ran down fly balls in the outfield, and stole two bases.

"I was impressed that he played so hard," said Rantz. The scout alerted the Minnesota team to this impressive performance. He continued to follow Puckett's progress. The more Rantz and the Twins' officials saw of Puckett, the more they believed that this late bloomer had a special gift for the game. On January 12, 1982, they selected Puckett in the first round of the free agent draft. The kid who had been passed over completely in past years was the third person chosen in the entire draft. In less than two years Kirby Puckett had jumped from a "can't-make-it" to a "can't miss" prospect.

Chapter 3

Puckett was thrilled to be given a chance to play with the pros. But eager as he was to get going on his career, he decided to stick it out at Triton through the year. His college grades had not been good. Puckett did not want to leave school on a low note. "I wanted to prove to myself that I could go to school."

Puckett raised his grades. Meanwhile he tore up the opposition for his Triton team. He batted a sizzling .472 and belted 16 home runs. He stole 42 bases and threw out 23 runners on the base paths. As soon as the college season was finished, Puckett joined the Twins' organization. By all outward appearances he breezed through his first minor league experiences at Elizabethton, Tennessee. During his 65 games there he batted .382 and stole 43 bases. He led the Appalachian League in seven categories. In 1983 Puckett was moved up to Visalia in the California League. There he batted .314, drove in 97 runs, and was voted the league's best major league baseball prospect. The Twins' owner, Calvin Griffith, was so certain of Puckett's talent that he often mentioned the youngster as a star of the future.

But despite all these impressive numbers, Puckett's confidence was shaky. Sometimes his insecurity actually helped him to keep improving. For example Puckett's arm was strong enough to throw out 22 base-runners in 138 games at Visalia. Yet Puckett thought he needed to improve. When the season ended, he attended an off-season instructional league to learn how to get more power behind his throws.

One phase of his game, however, really suffered from lack of confidence—his power hitting. The Twins had expected their number one draft choice to hit home runs as well as base hits. But Puckett's power seemed to slip away in the minor leagues. He hit only 9 home runs in 548 at bats while playing for Visalia. The problem was that Puckett had come to believe that he could not pull the ball against fast-throwing professional hurlers. Rather than swinging hard at their pitches, he was just trying to make contact. He slapped at the ball and sprayed singles just over the infielders' heads. This gave him a high batting average, but few extra base hits.

Ever since Cesar Tovar had left the Twins in 1973, the team had been searching for a good lead-off batter. They had been counting on young Jim Eisenreich to claim both the center field position and the leadoff spot. Eisenreich had played brilliantly in the minors and in brief stints with the Twins. There was no doubt that he could hit major league pitching.

Unfortunately Eisenreich's career was halted by an unusual nervous disorder. A month into the 1984 season the Twins discovered that they needed to find a new center fielder and leadoff hitter. For lack of a better solution, they considered Kirby Puckett. Puckett had been assigned to the Twins' top farm club, the Toledo Mud Hens. In 21 games with Toledo, Puckett had batted only .263 and shown even less power than he had in the lower minor leagues.

Twins' officials debated bringing Puckett up to the majors. Sure he ran fast, worked hard, and was an excellent fielder. But could he hit big league pitching? Was he ready to face hard-throwing people like Jack Morris, Rick Langston, and Dave Stieb? Unable to come up with a better solution to their problem, the Twins' management called up Puckett.

On May 8, 1984, major-league fans got their first look at one of the most unusual ballplayers they had ever seen. From a distance the 5-foot, 8-inch, 180-pound Puckett looked like a chubby little kid. His warm smile and eager, enthusiastic nature made him seem too lovable to be a real competitor.

California Angels' slugger Reggie Jackson sized up the newcomer who was taking his pre-game warm-ups in Anaheim Stadium. Puckett did not look like most lean, graceful major leaguers. But Jackson could see the power in those thick legs and shoulders. Not quite sure what to make of the rookie, the outgoing Jackson decided to ask. He walked over to Puckett and said, "You look pretty strong. You hit the long ball?"

Puckett could hardly believe he was actually talking to the great Reggie Jackson. "No, I don't, Mr. Jackson," Puckett admitted.

"You don't hit the long ball?" Jackson studied the rookie again. "You look like you should."

"No, I'm just a base-hitter, Mr. Jackson," Puckett insisted.

The Twins sent Puckett up to the plate to lead off the game against California's veteran right-hander, Jim Slaton. For Puckett it was the thrill of a lifetime. He could hardly wait for the first pitch to reach the plate.

"I was real nervous," said Puckett. "I hit a bullet up the hole and they threw me out." As he trotted back to the dugout, he thought about how much tougher it was to get a hit in the major leagues. He was sure that the infielders he had played

No one had to ask Reggie Jackson if he hit the long ball. The swing tells it all.

against in the minor leagues would never have gotten to that ball.

But everything fell into place for the rest of the game. Puckett pounded out four more hits that the California fielders could not reach. "Before I knew it, I was four for five," Puckett said. "Then it all looked like a piece of cake." After one game in the majors, Puckett was batting .800! Those four hits tied an American League record for hits in a player's first game.

American League pitchers quickly brought Puckett back to earth. Kirby managed only one single in five at bats in his second game. But he continued to hit well enough to hold on to his leadoff spot in the Twins' lineup.

Puckett finished the season with an excellent .296 batting mark. He also stole 16 bases, covered a lot of ground in the outfield, and caught the ball well. In addition, the rookie threw out sixteen base runners who tested his throwing arm.

There was still, however, that glaring weakness in the newcomer's performance. Puckett had more than lived up to his own billing as a singles hitter. In fact, despite his weightlifter's build, Kirby Puckett had proved to be one of the most powderpuff hitters in the league. Only 17 of his 165 hits in 1984 went for extra bases. He failed to hit one home run the entire season.

Puckett swung a little bit harder during his second season. On April 22, 1985, in his 613th major league at bat, he finally hit a ball over the fence. Some of his line drive hits began to find the gaps in the outfield for doubles and triples.

Yet opposing teams knew they had little to fear from Puckett's bat. Every pitcher in the league knew that Puckett could not pull the ball to the third base side of the field. All he was trying to do was get his bat on the ball and slap it through the right side of the infield.

Managers then began shifting their infielders to take advantage of Puckett's weakness as a hitter. The outfielders moved in closer and toward right field. Shortstops moved over to the first base side of second. Before long there was little room for Puckett's slap hits to get through. Puckett's batting average dropped to .288 in his second season.

Puckett had reached a critical stage in his career. Opponents had caught on to him. They would make it more and more difficult for him to slap singles through the right side. If Puckett could not find some way to adjust he would probably never be much better than an ordinary big league hitter. The Twins had expected much more from this stocky strongman. In nearly 1,250 major league at bats during his two seasons, Puckett had managed just 4 home runs. What could he do to break out of his "singles-hitter" mold?

Even when the Twins struggle, Puckett keeps a positive attitude.

Chapter 4

Reggie Jackson was not the only baseball person confused by the mystery of Puckett's weak swing. Old-timers noted how much Puckett reminded them of slugger Hack Wilson, who played in the 1930s. Standing only 5 feet, 6 inches, with a bull neck and thick shoulders, Wilson had once hit 54 home runs in a season. Playing for the Chicago Cubs in 1930, he had set a major league record by driving in 190 runs. Yet Puckett, with an almost identical squatty build, rarely hit a ball as far as the warning track.

In spring training of 1986 Puckett sought help from the Twins' batting coach, Tony Oliva. Before his career was cut short by injuries, Oliva had been one of the hardest hitters in baseball. Puckett was willing to listen to any advice the former master might give.

Oliva liked what he saw of Puckett's quick, level stroke. But he could see that Kirby was not getting his weight into his swing. Puckett was so anxious to hit the ball that he was swinging early. He would step into the pitch before it reached the plate. By the time the ball arrived, his weight was already

With a body build similar to Puckett's Chicago Cub mini-brute Hack Wilson pounded out 56 homeruns and a major league record 190 RBIs in 1930.

on his forward foot. Instead of shifting his weight smoothly, Puckett often ended up making an off-balance lunge. It was like trying to swing while standing on one foot. No wonder the man could not hit for power.

Puckett knew exactly why he was swinging so early. "I didn't want them to throw the ball by me," he admitted. Oliva helped Puckett to gain enough confidence in himself to wait a little longer on each pitch. To help him keep his weight back, Oliva had his student kick his left foot in the air at the start of the swing.

Oliva saw another reason why Puckett could not pull the ball to left field. Kirby did not like to hit inside pitches. To keep pitchers from throwing inside against him, he stood far away from the plate. Oliva pointed out that you cannot pull the ball if you are trying to hit everything off the end of your bat. The coach moved Puckett closer to the plate. Then he showed him some techniques for hitting inside pitches. Before long Puckett was learning to jerk those inside pitches into left field.

The Twins were pleased with Puckett's progress in spring training. They believed that he could hit 15 to 18 home runs a year if he followed Oliva's advice and did not go back to lunging. But neither they nor the opposing American League pitchers were prepared for the fireworks Puckett put on in 1986. The Twins' center fielder smashed eight home runs in the first month of the season—twice as many as he had in his first two full seasons in the majors! At the same time he slashed enough singles and doubles to hit .396 during that first month of the season.

Shell-shocked pitchers groped for new ways to get Puckett out now that the old methods no longer worked. Puckett pounded everything they threw at him. In early May he faced Detroit Tiger pitcher Walt Terrell. Puckett smacked the first

Demonstrating what he learned from batting coach Tony Oliva, Puckett gets all of his weight into a pitch (above) and enjoys the result (below).

pitch of the game into the stands for his 11th home run in 24 games. The "singles-hitter" was now belting home runs at a rate that would shatter Roger Maris's single-season record if he kept up this pace.

At first Puckett acted as surprised as everyone else at what he was doing. It was as though his bat had turned into a magic wand. "This is like a dream," he said. But after a few weeks Puckett began to realize that the sizzling line drives off his bats were not just due to an outrageous streak of luck. He really did have the power to be a major league home-run hitter.

The early season power surge boosted his confidence. In one game against New York, Puckett whacked three long fly balls into center field. The drives would have sailed out of most ballparks in the league. But they could not quite reach the fence in Yankee Stadium's spacious center field. All three balls were caught.

Puckett returned to the bench after the third long out feeling discouraged. Manager Ray Miller advised him to hit the ball to another part of the field. "This park's too big for you," commented Miller.

Instead of listening to his manager's advice, though, Puckett took it as a challenge. In the very next game Puckett stepped up to the plate and launched another tremendous shot straight to center field. This one sailed over the fence, landing more than 440 feet from home plate. On returning to the dugout Puckett could not resist needling his manager. "There's your 'too big,' Skip!" said Puckett.

Kirby slacked off a little from his scorching early pace. But he left no doubt that he was the Twins' batting star of the future. Puckett finished the season with 31 home runs, 37 doubles, and 98 runs batted in. By learning to hit the ball to all fields, Puckett collected 223 hits and raised his batting

Puckett accepts congratulations after hitting his seventh home run in just 19 games in April 1986.

average to .328. The Twins' new star finished second in the American League in both hits and runs scored, and was awarded a Golden Glove as the league's best defensive center fielder.

Such all-around skill reminded many baseball fans of Puckett's old hero, Willie Mays. But his great effort for a struggling team reminded others of another Puckett hero, Ernie Banks. Despite Banks's Hall of Fame effort, his teams lost far more often than they won. Yet Banks showed up at the park every day with a smile on his face, delighted just to be playing ball.

Puckett seemed to have been cast in the same mold. Even his tremendous performance could not lift the Twins to a winning season. They finished with a dismal 71–91 record. After three years in the big leagues Puckett had yet to play on a team with a winning record. But rather than get discouraged, Puckett continued to bubble over with enthusiasm. He loved playing baseball. He loved living in his new city of

Kirby and wife Tonya try to stay warm as they ride in a parade through the Twin Cities.

Minneapolis. And he loved his girlfriend, Tonya, whom he would marry in November 1986. In the midst of a losing situation Puckett held his head up and kept smiling.

Minnesota made a few moves to improve its team for 1987. The most important change was the arrival of relief specialist Jeff Reardon from the Montreal Expos to patch up the Twins' weak bullpen. Yet baseball experts saw little hope for any great improvement. Most pegged the Twins as a middle-of-the-pack team that would not challenge for the divisional title.

Nonetheless Kirby Puckett could hardly wait for winter to be over so he could get back to the fun of playing baseball. As usual he got down to Florida at the first opportunity to get ready for the new season. If the Twins failed to improve, it would not be because Puckett was coasting on his success.

Chapter 5

Minnesota hired Tom Kelly to take over as manager in 1987. Kelly believed in combining hard practices with a relaxed, easygoing team spirit. Kirby Puckett was perfectly suited to Kelly's style of managing. He loved to practice. He would often show up in the locker room at 2:30 p.m. to start getting himself ready for a 7 p.m. game. Other players on the team could not resent long, grueling hours on the practice field when the team's star was practicing harder than anyone.

At the same time Puckett helped Kelly keep the Twins relaxed and enthusiastic. Puckett was not a take-charge, holler-type of guy. He left that kind of leadership to others such as third baseman Gary Gaetti. Puckett preferred to lead by example. It was difficult for players to get big heads about their skills or get jealous of each other when the team's star stayed so humble. Puckett was so friendly and fun to be around that rookies and free agents immediately felt comfortable around him. One player simply summed up Puckett's effect on the team. "Everyone loves Kirby."

Tom Kelly agreed that Puckett's team value went far

Puckett performs one of the duties that come with being a baseball hero—signing autographs.

beyond his batting and fielding statistics. "There's something about the guy that just makes you feel good."

With Kelly's guidance, veteran leadership, and Puckett's example, the Twins played enthusiastically in 1987. Opposing players commented that the Twins seemed to be having more fun than most other teams. At the same time Minnesota began beating some of its more highly ranked rivals.

Now that Puckett was blasting the ball all over the park, Kelly changed the batting lineup to make better use of Kirby's batting skill. He switched the center fielder from the lead-off spot to third in the batting order. That gave Puckett a chance to come to bat with runners on base so that he could drive them in. Puckett did not let Kelly down. He repeatedly drove in important runs as the Twins burst off to a surprising start.

Twins' fans appreciated the effort their team was putting out. The Twins' home park, the Hubert H. Humphrey Metrodome, began filling with noisy fans eager to cheer their team on to victory. Backed by this support the Twins played well at home. But they continued to struggle when playing on the road. Still in late August, the Minnesota Twins were hanging tough in the American League Western Division race.

Whenever the Twins needed that extra spark in 1987, Puckett came through. He enjoyed playing defense as much as he enjoyed batting, and he patrolled the outfield with confidence. While opposing center fielders struggled to find high fly balls against the white background of the Metrodome, Puckett routinely chased them down. He soared high above the fence to rob a batter of a home run so often that he made the play look routine. Base runners had learned their lesson about testing Puckett's arm. After throwing out 37 runners in his first two years, Puckett seldom got a chance to gun down anyone in 1987. He totaled only 8 outfield assists that season, mainly because most runners would not take chances with him.

As a batter Puckett could carry the team for several games at a time. When they traveled to Milwaukee in late August, the Twins' offense was in a slump. With Minnesota fading fast, the powerful Oakland A's were poised to take control of the division race. That was when Puckett swatted his record-setting 10 hits in two games to batter the Brewers and recharge the Twins.

As the Twins continued their winning ways at home, the rest of the American League West dropped off the pace. The surprising Twins hung on to win the division with an unspectacular 85–77 record. Again it was Puckett who led the Twins' offensive attack with statistics almost identical to his great 1986 season. Puckett cracked out 207 hits for a .332 batting average. He continued to hit for power, clouting 28 homers. Batting in the key number three spot in the order, he knocked in 99 runs.

The Twins' divisional victory was dismissed as a fluke caused by the team's unusual home field advantage. Fifty-six of Minnesota's wins had come in the friendly environment of its home dome. The horrible record of 29–52 on the road left many questioning whether they were a deserving playoff team. But the Twins had posted the best mark in its division and so were entitled to battle the Detroit Tigers in the American League Championship Series.

Pumped up by thunderous noise from their home fans, the Twins' players surprised the favored Tigers by winning the first game, 8–5. While Gaetti grabbed the headlines with two home runs, Puckett made his own quiet contribution. With the Twins trailing 5–4 in the eighth inning, he doubled to drive in Dan Gladden, fueling the game-winning rally. Minnesota also won game two of the series. The team did it without much help from its star center fielder, who went hitless.

The series then moved to Detroit, where Puckett continued to struggle at the plate. This time his teammates were unable to make up for his quiet bat. Detroit won game three. Again the critics wrote off the Twins as a team that could not win away from home. Game four of the series was crucial. The Twins had ridden into the series on a wave of emotion. Supercharged with enthusiasm the Minnesota players had overwhelmed the Tigers in the first two games. But by winning game three, the Tigers had put the brakes on the Twins' title charge. Now the more experienced Tigers, playing at home, were in a good position to take charge of the series.

This time Kirby Puckett came out swinging. He erased an early Detroit lead with a third-inning home run. He then drove in another run to help the Twins pull out a tense, 5–3 win. Puckett added two more hits as the Twins hammered the Tigers in the final game of the series.

Detroit's veteran manager Sparky Anderson was impressed with the Twins' spirit. "The Twins came in here with more get up and go than ever I have played against in a playoff," he marveled. That enthusiasm put Puckett and the Twins in a place where almost no one had expected them to be—the World Series.

Just as in its playoff series, Minnesota burst out to a quick lead over the St. Louis Cardinals. Again the team managed just fine without much help from Puckett. Dan Gladden's grand slam home run broke open the first game. Puckett collected just one hit in that 10–1 win. He picked up another hit in game two, but he was not an important factor in the Twins' 8–4 win.

Again the Twins began to falter as soon as they left the roar of the Metrodome. The Minnesota bats went silent at St.

Louis' Busch Stadium. Puckett managed only one single in three official at bats in game three. The Twins lost, 3–1. Although Puckett finally drove in a run with an infield single in game four, he went hitless in his three other at bats. And Minnesota lost, 7–2.

Cardinal pitchers completely tied up Puckett in game five. With two men on and no one out in the eighth inning, Puckett flied out to center field. The Twins' ace hitter went 0 for 4 as the Twins lost again. The unlikely thrill ride of Minnesota seemed over. The Cardinals were on a roll and needed to win only one of the last two games in Minnesota.

By this time Puckett was feeling the pressure. In five World Series games he had managed only four singles in 20 at

Even opponents can't help smiling around Kirby. St. Louis third baseman Terry Pendleton shares a light moment with the Twins' star before their World Series match.

bats. That came out to a .200 average—far below the usual Puckett numbers. Kirby was confused by his failure. He knew that the Cardinals' pitchers were getting him out by throwing the ball inside at him. But he could not seem to adjust. The more the Twins needed him to come through with a big hit, the worse he swung. He was getting so anxious at the plate that he was thrown off his rhythm.

As usual when Puckett needed batting advice he sought out Tony Oliva. Puckett worked with his coaches on extra batting practice before game six. Time after time he had pitchers keep throwing the ball in on his hands.

The extra practice paid off in game six. Puckett burst out of his mini-slump with a run-scoring single in the first. He went on to collect three more solid hits, plus a walk. Paced by Kirby's World Series record of four runs scored in one game, the Twins came from behind to win the game and tie the series.

The deciding game was a tense affair with many close calls on the bases. Puckett came to the plate in the fifth inning with the Twins trailing 2–1. He slashed a double into the gap between right and center fields to score Gagne and knot the game. The Twins then went on to win the game, 4–2 behind the steady pitching of World Series Most Valuable Player, Frank Viola.

Incredibly the Minnesota Twins were the world champions of major league baseball. "We've overcome a lot of adversity," Puckett said amid a wild celebration afterward. "I think we surprised everyone but ourselves."

Chapter 6

Puckett and the Twins played even better the following year. But it takes luck as well as skill to win pennants. In 1988 Minnesota had the bad fortune to play in the same division as the most talented team of the decade. The Oakland A's, led by slugger Jose Canseco and pitchers Dave Stewart and Dennis Eckersley, shot off to a fast start that year. The Twins stayed close to the A's into August, waiting for Oakland to fade down the stretch. But Oakland never faded. Even though Minnesota won six more games than it had during its 1987 championship year, the team finished 13 games behind the streaking A's.

Kirby Puckett enjoyed the best year of his career in a losing cause. Smashing line shots to all fields, he waged a fierce battle with Boston Red Sox ace Wade Boggs for the batting title. Like all left-handed batters Boggs held a batting advantage over Puckett. Lefties stand a few steps closer to first base than right-handers. Those few steps often mean the difference between beating out an infield hit or being thrown out. But in early August Puckett edged past Boggs .357 to .355.

Wade Boggs, Puckett's main rival for the batting title.

Puckett struggled for a couple of weeks in early September. He recovered, though, and finished the season with a furious charge. In the final 17 games of the season Puckett batted over .450.

But it was not enough to catch the equally scorching Boggs. Boston's third baseman won his fourth straight batting title with a .366 average. Puckett's .356 average was still the best mark posted by a right-handed batter in nearly a half century. Historians had to go back to the great Joe DiMaggio's .357 in 1941 to find a higher average by a right-hander! Minnesota's "mini-brute" finished the year with 234 hits. That was the most by a right-handed batter in the American League since Al Simmons back in 1925! Puckett managed this feat without sacrificing any power. He swatted 24 home runs, 42 doubles, and drove in a career-high 121 runs.

Oakland continued to get stronger over the next few years. It added pitching ace Bob Welch and speedster Rickey Henderson. Even with Puckett anchoring the lineup, Minnesota could not compete with the A's. As the team tried to rebuild a new team to challenge Oakland, the Twins fell back into their old losing ways.

But whether in the thick of a pennant race or in a dreary season, Puckett produced the same peppy effort and the same impressive result. In 1989 he took another run at the American League batting title. With Boggs getting off to a slow start, Puckett found himself in a duel with Oakland's Carney Landsford, the 1982 batting champ. Puckett trailed Landsford by nearly 20 points in early June. But he kept his average steady, near the .340 mark, while Landsford started to slip. By August 1 Puckett's .339 average was good for a 10-point lead over Landsford.

The A's third baseman got back in the groove in

September, though. By mid-month, the two were even at .336 each. Puckett inched ahead and held a narrow lead going into the final two games of the season. Then disaster struck. Puckett could not figure out the pitches of Seattle's Bill Swift and went hitless in four at bats. That meant with one game to go, the two were locked in a virtual tie at .338.

On the final day of the season, the two were playing at the same time on the West Coast. Puckett would try his luck against Seattle's Eric Hanson, while Landsford was pitted against Kansas City's Tom Gordon. Kirby came through with two solid doubles in five at bats to raise his average to .339. Then he looked to see if his rival could top that.

He couldn't. Landsford went hitless in three at bats to drop to .336. Puckett had won the batting title. Landsford, although disappointed at the narrow loss, showed the respect that Puckett had gained among his fellow players. "He probably deserves it more than I do," Landsford said. "He puts those numbers up, 200 hits, every year."

By this time fans had come to expect so much of Puckett that some of them were actually disappointed in his season. They wondered why Puckett's home run production had dropped to only nine. Although he continued to show power with 45 doubles and a team-leading 85 runs batted in, some wondered if he was slipping back into his old singles-hitting ways.

Puckett heard the critics. "A lot of people said I was having a bad year because I didn't hit as many home runs," he said at the season's end. "But this is a tough game. Even the best players can't repeat their performances every season." Puckett had been such an outstanding all-around player that he could win a batting title, lead the league in hits, and still feel he had to apologize for his performance.

The Twins knew that Kirby had nothing to apologize for.

On November 23, 1989, Minnesota offered its star a three-year contract worth $9 million. That made Kirby the highest-paid player in baseball. Just one day later Orel Hershiser signed a contract for even more money. Players' salaries skyrocketed far above Puckett's earnings. Some stars complained when they found they were being passed in salary by lesser players. Puckett, though, just shrugged off talk about money. He stated that he had been thrilled to be the highest paid player for one day. He was making more money than he had ever thought possible as it was, so he had no reason to complain.

The 1990 season was a disaster for the Twins. Still trying to rebuild with younger players, the Minnesota team finished in last place. For the first time Puckett showed signs of wear and tear. That bulky body was taking its toll on his speed. Puckett stole only five bases. Although he was still the master

Puckett has lost a step or two from his rookie year, but is still a threat to steal a base when his team needs it.

at leaping catches on the warning track, he could not cover quite as much ground in the outfield as he used to. Even his batting suffered. For the first time in four seasons Puckett failed to top the .300 mark. But he had lost none of his enthusiasm or his popularity. The Metrodome echoed with cheers every time his name was announced.

The 1991 season started just as poorly for the Twins. Despite adding proven veterans, such as pitcher Jack Morris and designated hitter Chili Davis during the off-season, Minnesota staggered off to a 2–9 start. No one had predicted they would be contenders for the division title, but they were not supposed to be that bad either.

Still Puckett and the Twins kept a positive attitude. Puckett felt sure that if they kept working, playing hard, and having fun, things would change. Sure enough the Twins caught fire in June. A long winning streak that month put them in the thick of the divisional race. Shortly after the All-Star game in July, the Twins broke away from the pack and romped to the divisional title. That made them the first team in baseball history to go from last to first in one year. Puckett, too, had rebounded from a subpar season. He batted .319 and raised his home runs total to 15.

At the start of the Twins' American League Championship series against the Toronto Blue Jays, Puckett brushed off talk of playoff pressure. "We're not even supposed to be here in the playoffs," he said. Since no one expected anything of the Twins, he noted, the players could just relax and have some fun.

Yet those who interviewed Puckett could tell that he was still as excited as a rookie to get on the field for another championship series. He answered questions in a burst of nervous energy, his words spurting out machine-gun fast. He rarely told reporters anything new. Puckett was not one to sit back and calmly analyze the fine points of his craft. As far as he was concerned, the past was past. All he wanted to do was get up to the plate for another shot.

"You know me, man, I'm an aggressive hitter. I just go up there hacking, and we'll see what happens," he would say without taking a breath between sentences. Although polite and cooperative, he seemed as though he could hardly wait to get the words out of the way and get out on the field. After all these years Puckett was still far more comfortable playing the game he loved than talking about it.

As usual the excitable Puckett had trouble settling into a rhythm in the opening playoff game against Toronto. He went hitless in four at bats, and did not contribute to the Twins' win. In game two, after three tries, he managed one hit, a run-single, off Jose Guzman. Toronto, however, broke the Twins homefield playoff magic with a 4–2 win.

In 1987 Puckett had started slowly in the playoffs without attracting much attention. But by this time he had become such a popular figure that everything he did came under close inspection. Sportswriters pestered him about his failure to hit. Puckett could not understand what the fuss was about. He pointed out that the teams had played only two games and he was not swinging badly. He did not plan to do anything differently; he would just go up there "hacking" and wait for the hits to fall.

Sure enough the hits started to fall in game three in Toronto. Puckett pounded out two hits, including a double, and drove in a run in the Twins' victory. Puckett was getting comfortable at the plate and that spelled trouble for Toronto. In game four the Blue Jays jumped out to a 1–0 lead against the Twins' ace Jack Morris. But Puckett had evened the score with one mighty swing in the fourth inning. His lead-off home run landed 426 feet away in center field! Kirby then slammed

Never one to panic when the hits aren't falling, Puckett just "goes up there hacking."

two more hits and drove in another run as the Twins won easily.

The Blue Jays made a determined bid to rally in game five. But it was Puckett who sent them packing for home. He led off the Twins' scoring with a home run. Then in the eighth inning, with the score tied at 5–5, he broke open the game with a bases-loaded single. Puckett had answered critics' doubts with 8 hits in his final 13 at bats. His .429 average, 2 homers, and 6 crucial runs batted in easily earned him the Most Valuable Player Award for the American League Championship Series.

Chapter 7

Like the Twins the surprising Atlanta Braves had charged up from a last place finish in 1990 to capture its league championship in 1991. The team's deep pitching staff had shut out the Pittsburgh Pirates three times to earn a trip to the World Series. The Braves posed a stiff challenge to the Twins, who were hoping to repeat their astounding title run of 1987.

Kirby Puckett suffered through his usual first-game jitters at the Metrodome. Veteran Charlie Liebrandt took advantage of his impatience. Slow change-ups left Puckett hitting nothing but air during his first two at bats. He failed to hit in four trips to the plate, but his teammates came through to win the game. Puckett floundered even more in the second game. He killed a Twins' rally in the first inning by hitting into a double play. Then Kirby went hitless the rest of the game. Fortunately Scott Leius clouted a late-inning home run to gain the victory.

Minnesota moved to Atlanta to try its luck against the Braves' brilliant young star Steve Avery. Unhittable in recent weeks Avery had shut out the Pirates twice in the playoffs. He was not the sort of pitcher that most batters want to face when stuck in a slump. Puckett, however, had learned not to be intimidated by pitchers. When he was asked to name the toughest pitcher in the majors, Puckett had simply said, "None." The most important thing was for him to get into a comfortable rhythm at the plate. If he could do that, he could hit off anybody.

Puckett paid no attention to Avery's reputation. In fact he jolted the stylish lefty by clouting a home run off him. In the late innings Puckett had a chance to tie the game. With a man on third base and only one out, all he needed to do was hit a fly ball to score a run. Instead Puckett's eagerness got the best of him. He chased a high fastball and struck out, leaving the runner stranded. The Braves ended up winning a thriller in the bottom of the twelfth inning.

After the game the always upbeat Puckett shrugged off his disappointment. "I've chased bad pitches before," he said. Apparently he was not impressed with his home run. Talking about his troubles at the plate, he said, "All I have to do is hit one ball hard. Then maybe I'll remember how to do it."

Unfortunately nothing jogged his memory in the next two games. Puckett went 2 for 6, but was unable to provide a key hit. Minnesota lost both games. Just like in 1987 the team returned home for the final two games, needing to win both in order to take the World Series.

Puckett's pride had been stung just as it had been in the first five games of the 1987 World Series. His totals against Atlanta showed 3 hits in 18 at bats for a .167 average. He did have the one home run, but that did not make up for the wasted opportunities. To make matters worse Twins' power hitters Kent Hrbek and Shane Mack seemed totally handcuffed. Now Atlanta was sending out Steve Avery against the Twins' slumping Scott Erickson. Everything

A gleeful Puckett pounces on pitching ace Jack Morris as the Twins celebrate a World Series win.

seemed to be in Atlanta's favor. The Twins needed the real Kirby Puckett to show up for game six to have any chance at all.

Puckett came through with one of most incredible all-around shows in World Series history. He continued to pound Avery, ripping a triple down the third base line in the first inning to score a run. In the top of the third, Atlanta's Ron Gant blasted Scott Erickson's pitch deep into center field. Puckett drifted back to the fence. He soared high into the air, incredibly high for a man with his bulk. He seemed to hang in the air like Michael Jordan. At the peak of his leap he snatched the ball just before it struck off the plexiglass fence. The catch saved at least one run and probably several more. Puckett had no explanation for the astounding catch. As he explained later, "It's something you can't practice. It just happens."

In the bottom half of the inning Puckett was again up with a man on third. This time he drove a fly ball deep to the outfield to score the runner easily.

But despite Kirby's one-man show, the Twins could not shake the determined Braves. For the third time in four games, the contest went into extra innings. Neither team scored in the tenth. The Braves could not push across a run in the eleventh. But Minnesota fans sensed danger. Desperate to keep the Braves from scoring, Tom Kelly had brought ace reliever Rick Aguilera into the game early. Aguilera had given them about all the innings they could expect out of him. If the Twins did not score in the eleventh, they were in trouble.

The Braves turned the ball over to veteran Charlie Liebrandt, who had made Puckett look so foolish in game one. Puckett reminded himself not to get too anxious at the plate. Liebrandt was a master at getting hitters to chase low pitches that spun out of the strike zone. "I just wanted to make him get the ball up," Puckett explained.

Puckett rounds third base after his dramatic game-winning homer in game six of the 1991 World Series.

This time Puckett stayed under control. He laid off two tempting pitches that curved away from the plate. With the count two balls and one strike, Liebrandt tried to keep Puckett off balance with a slow change-up. Puckett was ready for it. The man who may be, pound for pound, the strongest man in baseball stepped into the pitch and drove it deep to the outfield.

Puckett usually controls his excitement while out on the field. But as he saw the ball disappear over the fence and heard the deafening roar, he let loose with howls of joy. He stabbed his fist in the air. When his team had most needed him, he had carried the team on his shoulders for an entire game and taken them to victory. "Unbelievable!" gasped Puckett in the dugout. When asked if he was getting any rest at all in this heart-stopping series, he gave them the Kirby Puckett philosophy, "I'll get my rest when I'm dead."

Game seven was even more gut-wrenching than the other games. Atlanta pitcher John Smolz dueled the Twins' Morris for inning after scoreless inning. Both teams put a winning run on third base, with just one out, only to come up short.

The Braves had seen all they needed to of Kirby Puckett's heroics. They were determined that he was not going to beat them in this final game. Atlanta walked Puckett three times. He could only stand and watch as Gene Larkin came to the plate with the bases loaded and one out.

He saw Larkin's hit to the opposite field drop in behind the Atlanta outfield to score Dan Gladden with the winning run. The Twins had come out on top in what many considered the most exciting World Series of all time.

Kirby Puckett had single-handedly kept the series alive for that seventh game. Even before his World Series heroics he had been the most popular Twins' player in history. He had been constantly swamped by autograph requests and hounded

The most popular Twin in team history salutes his fans.

by fans wherever he went. After his stunning sixth-game home run, Kirby was fast becoming a legend. Yet his teammates were far from jealous of the affection he commanded.

Infielder Al Newman, who joined Puckett in shaving his head for luck, called him "the eighth wonder of the world." Kent Hrbek, the Twins' slugger who had grown up near Minnesota's old stadium, felt no resentment toward the man who had taken his hometown by storm. "It's a joy to go up to the plate after he hits and listen to the catcher talk about how he was able to hit a certain pitch," said Hrbek.

Puckett commanded the same type of respect from opposing players as well. The week after Minnesota's 1991 World Series win Puckett sponsored a pool-shooting tournament in Minneapolis to raise money for the Children's Heart Fund. The cause was especially dear to Kirby since both of his parents had died of heart disease. Puckett asked a number of All-Star ballplayers to help him with his tournament.

Unfortunately Minneapolis was hit with a monster snowstorm the weekend of the tournament. With 28 inches of snow falling in one day, transportation was a nightmare. It would have been foolish for players to try to make it through. Yet, somehow a host of players such as Bobby Bonilla, Cal Ripken, Jr., Joe Carter, and Eddie Murray braved the storm and showed up. All were willing to make the extra effort to be there in support of Puckett.

Minnesota general manager Andy McPhail has been around major league baseball all of his life. He has seen a lot of superstars come and go, replaced by new stars. But he knows that Kirby Puckett is one of those rare players who can never be replaced. "It's your dying wish as a general manager that he's always going to be part of your ballclub."

Career Statistics

Year	Team	G	AB	R	H	2B	3B	HR	RBI	SB	AVG
1982	Elizabethton*	65	275	65	105	15	3	3	35	43	.382
1983	Visalia*	548	138	105	172	29	7	9	97	48	.314
1984	Toledo*	21	80	9	21	2	0	1	5	8	.263
1984	Minnesota	128	557	63	165	12	5	0	31	14	.296
1985	Minnesota	161	691	80	199	29	13	4	74	21	.288
1986	Minnesota	161	680	119	223	37	6	31	96	20	.328
1987	Minnesota	157	624	96	207	32	5	28	99	12	.332
1988	Minnesota	158	657	109	234	42	5	24	121	6	.356
1989	Minnesota	159	635	75	215	45	4	9	85	11	.339
1990	Minnesota	146	551	82	164	40	3	12	80	5	.298
1991	Minnesota	152	611	92	195	29	6	15	89	11	.319
1992	Minnesota	160	639	104	210	38	4	19	110	17	.329
Major League Totals		1382	5645	820	1812	304	51	142	785	107	.321

*Minor Leagues

Where to Write Kirby Puckett:

Mr. Kirby Puckett
c/o Minnesota Twins
501 Chicago Ave. South
Minneapolis, MN 55415

Index

Leius, Scott, 53, 56

M
Mack, Shane, 54
Maris, Roger, 31
Mays, Willie, 16, 33
McPhail, Andy, 60
Miller, Ray, 31
Milwaukee Brewers, 7, 38
Milwaukee County Stadium, 7
Minneapolis, 14, 34
Montreal Expos, 34
Morris, Jack, 22, 48, 49, 58
Murray, Eddie, 60

N
Newman, Al, 60
Nieve, Juan, 8

O
Oakland A's, 8, 38, 43, 45
Oliva, Tony, 8, 27, 29, 41

P
Pittsburgh Pirates, 53
Plesac, Dan, 9
Puckett, Tonya, 34

R
Rantz, Jim, 19
Rantz, Mike, 19
Reardon, Jeff, 34
Ripken, Cal, Jr., 60
Robert Taylor homes, 14–16

S
St. Louis Cardinals, 39–41
Simmons, Al, 45
Slaton, Tim, 22
Smoltz, John, 58
spring training, 11, 27, 29, 34
Steib, Dave, 22
Steward, Dave, 43
Swift, Bill, 46

T
Terrell, Walt, 29

Toledo Mud Hens, 21
Toronto Blue Jays, 48, 49, 51
Tovar, Cesar, 21
Triton Community College, 19

U
U.S. Census Bureau, 17

V
Viola, Frank, 41
Visalia, California, 20, 21

W
Welch, Bob, 45
Will, George, 11
Williams, Billy, 16
Williams, Dick, 13
Wilson, Hack, 27
World Series, 1987, 39–41
World Series, 1991, 53–58

Y
Yankee Stadium, 31
Yount, Robin, 8